by Iain Gray

Lang**Syne**

PUBLISHING

WRITING *to* REMEMBER

LangSyne

PUBLISHING

WRITING *to* REMEMBER

79 Main Street, Newtongrange,
Midlothian EH22 4NA
Tel: 0131 344 0414   Fax: 0845 075 6085
E-mail: info@lang-syne.co.uk
www.langsyneshop.co.uk

Design by Dorothy Meikle
Printed by Ricoh Print Scotland

ISBN 978-1-85217-461-3

Baillie

MOTTO:
What is brighter than the stars?
(and)
It shines in the darkness
(and)
Virtue is greater than splendour.

CREST:
A boar's head.

NAME variations include:
Bailey
Bailie
Bailley
Bayley
Baly
Ballye
Bayllie
Bayly

Echoes of a far distant past
can still be found in most names

Chapter one:

Origins of Scottish surnames

by George Forbes

It all began with the Normans.

For it was they who introduced surnames into common usage more than a thousand years ago, initially based on the title of their estates, local villages and chateaux in France to distinguish and identify these landholdings, usually acquired at the point of a bloodstained sword.

Such grand descriptions also helped enhance the prestige of these arrogant warlords and generally glorify their lofty positions high above the humble serfs slaving away below in the pecking order who only had single names, often with Biblical connotations as in Pierre and Jacques.

The only descriptive distinctions among this peasantry concerned their occupations, like Pierre the swineherd or Jacques the ferryman.

The Normans themselves were originally Vikings (or Northmen) who raided, colonised and eventually settled down around the French coastline.

They had sailed up the Seine in their longboats in 900 AD under their ferocious leader Rollo and ruled the roost in north east France before sailing over to conquer England, bringing their relatively new tradition of having surnames with them.

It took another hundred years for the Normans to percolate northwards and surnames did not begin to appear in Scotland until the thirteenth century.

These adventurous knights brought an aura of chivalry with them and it was said no damsel of any distinction would marry a man unless he had at least two names.

The family names included that of Scotland's great hero Robert De Brus and his compatriots were warriors from families like the De Morevils, De Umphravils, De Berkelais, De Quincis, De Viponts and De Vaux.

As the knights settled the boundaries of their vast estates, they took territorial names, as in Hamilton, Moray, Crawford, Cunningham, Dunbar, Ross, Wemyss, Dundas, Galloway, Renfrew, Greenhill, Hazelwood, Sandylands and Church-hill.

Other names, though not with any obvious geographical or topographical features, nevertheless derived from ancient parishes like Douglas, Forbes, Dalyell and Guthrie.

Other surnames were coined in connection with occupations, castles or legendary deeds. Stuart originated in the word steward, a prestigious post which was an integral part of any large medieval household. The same applied to Cooks, Chamberlains, Constables and Porters.

Borders towns and forts – needed in areas like the Debateable Lands which were constantly fought over by feuding local families – had their own distinctive names; and it was often from them that the resident groups took their communal titles, as in the Grahams of Annandale, the Elliots and Armstrongs of the East Marches, the Scotts and Kerrs of Teviotdale and Eskdale.

Even physical attributes crept into surnames, as in Small, Little and More (the latter being 'beg' in Gaelic), Long or Lang, Stark, Stout, Strong or Strang and even Jolly.

Mieklejohns would have had the strength of several men, while Littlejohn was named after the legendary sidekick of Robin Hood.

Colours got into the act with Black, White, Grey, Brown and Green (Red developed into Reid,

Ruddy or Ruddiman). Blue was rare and nobody ever wanted to be associated with yellow.

Pompous worthies took the name Wiseman, Goodman and Goodall.

Words intimating the sons of leading figures were soon affiliated into the language as in Johnson, Adamson, Richardson and Thomson, while the Norman equivalent of Fitz (from the French-Latin 'filius' meaning 'son') cropped up in Fitzmaurice and Fitzgerald.

The prefix 'Mac' was 'son of' in Gaelic and clans often originated with occupations – as in MacNab being sons of the Abbot, MacPherson and MacVicar being sons of the minister and MacIntosh being sons of the chief.

The church's influence could be found in the names Kirk, Clerk, Clarke, Bishop, Friar and Monk. Proctor came from a church official, Singer and Sangster from choristers, Gilchrist and Gillies from Christ's servant, Mitchell, Gilmory and Gilmour from servants of St Michael and Mary, Malcolm from a servant of Columba and Gillespie from a bishop's servant.

The rudimentary medical profession was represented by Barber (a trade which also once included dentistry and surgery) as well as Leech or Leitch.

Businessmen produced Merchants, Mercers, Monypennies, Chapmans, Sellers and Scales, while down at the old village watermill the names that cropped up included Miller, Walker and Fuller.

Other self explanatory trades included Coopers, Brands, Barkers, Tanners, Skinners, Brewsters and Brewers, Tailors, Saddlers, Wrights, Cartwrights, Smiths, Harpers, Joiners, Sawyers, Masons and Plumbers.

Even the scenery was utilised as in Craig, Moor, Hill, Glen, Wood and Forrest.

Rank, whether high or low, took its place with Laird, Barron, Knight, Tennant, Farmer, Husband, Granger, Grieve, Shepherd, Shearer and Fletcher.

The hunt and the chase supplied Hunter, Falconer, Fowler, Fox, Forrester, Archer and Spearman.

The renowned medieval historian Froissart, who eulogised about the romantic deeds of chivalry (and who condemned Scotland as being a poverty stricken wasteland), once sniffily dismissed the peasantry of his native France as the jacquerie (or the jacques-without-names) but it was these same humble folk who ended up overthrowing the arrogant aristocracy.

In the olden days, only the blueblooded knights of antiquity were entitled to full, proper names, both Christian and surnames, but with the passing of time and a more egalitarian, less feudal atmosphere, more respectful and worthy titles spread throughout the populace as a whole.

Echoes of a far distant past can still be found in most names and they can be borne with pride in commemoration of past generations who fought and toiled in some capacity or other to make our nation what it now is, for good or ill.

Chapter two:

Patriotic causes

Derived from the Latin *baiulus*, which became *bailli* in Old French, Baillie and its popular spelling variant Bailey is an occupational surname denoting a porter, steward or civic official.

Until the post was abolished under local government reorganisation in Scotland in 1975, a 'baillie', or 'bailey', was the equivalent of the English 'magistrate', or 'alderman', and survives north of the border today only as a courtesy title.

However, although primarily an occupational surname, it is thought that it may also have developed as a 'location' surname – the location in question being the rural French community of Bailleul-En-Vimeu, near Abbeville, in Normandy.

Another particularly intriguing theory, although it should be stressed there is no firm evidence to support it, is that the ancestors of some Baillies of today may originally have been 'Balliols'.

It is thought that some original bearers of the Baillol name may have changed it to 'Baillie' in order to distance themselves from what was seen at the time as the shame of the hapless Scottish monarch John Balliol.

History has certainly not been kind to this much-ridiculed king of Scots.

In what is known as the Great Cause – the highly complex deliberations to decide who was entitled to take over the throne of Scotland following the death of the infant heir to the throne, Margaret, the Maid of Norway, in 1290 – Scottish nobles turned to England's Edward I for a solution.

For reasons that best suited his own dynastic ambitions, he ruled that John Balliol was the rightful heir – but Balliol became a mere tool of the arrogant and all-powerful Edward, better known to posterity as 'Hammer of the Scots.'

Balliol eventually launched what proved to be an abortive and disastrous rebellion against the humiliating position in which both he and the Scottish nation had been placed – only to end up being stripped of all his honours and titles by Edward.

This led to him being dubbed 'Toom Tabard', meaning 'empty cloak', and signifying someone of no power or substance, by his equally humiliated Scottish subjects.

It was left to the likes of the great freedom

fighter Sir William Wallace and, later, the warrior king Robert the Bruce to restore Scotland's honour in what is known as the Wars of Scottish Independence.

Whatever the origins of the Baillie name, what is known with certainty is that it was present in Scotland from earliest times.

A William de Bailli, or Baillie, is first recorded in Lothian in 1311, and it is from him that the prominent Lanarkshire families of the Baillies of Lamington and the Baillies of Jerviswood descend – in addition to the Baillies of Polkemmet, West Lothian, and the Baillies of Dochfour and Dunain, in the Inverness area.

Of Anglo-Norman roots, William de Baillie, of Hoperig, in Berwickshire, was granted the Lamington lands by David II.

Baillie had fought at his side in October of 1346 at the battle of Neville's Cross, near Durham, a conflict that ended not only in a decisive defeat for the Scots but also in the wounding and capture of David.

It was not until eleven years later that the monarch was released and allowed to return to his native Scotland.

In the following century, Alexander Baillie, of the Baillies of Lamington, was granted the lands of Dochfour and Dunain, in the area of Inverness, for his support of the royalist cause at the battle of Brechin.

Fought in May of 1452 just over two miles from the town of Brechin, in the northeast of Scotland, it was part of vicious civil war in which the powerful Black Douglases and other nobles who included Alexander Lindsay, 4th Earl of Crawford and also known as the Tiger Earl, were arrayed against James for control of the kingdom.

A royalist army led on the king's behalf by George Gordon, 2nd Earl of Huntly, and that included Alexander Baillie in its ranks, defeated the rebel forces led by the Tiger Earl.

It was in reward for his services that the Earl of Huntly granted Alexander Baillie the lands of Dochfour and Dunain and also appointed him Constable of Inverness Castle.

But the fortunes of the Baillies went into decline after many of their lands were forfeited as punishment for their support of Mary, Queen of Scots at the battle of Langside.

The ill-starred Queen had earlier escaped

from Lochleven Castle, in which she had been imprisoned after being forced to sign her abdication, by a body known as the Confederate Lords.

A group of nine earls, nine bishops, 18 lairds, and others who included the Baillies signed a bond declaring their support for her, and both sides met at Langside, near Glasgow, on May 13, 1568.

Mary's forces, under the command of the Earl of Argyll, had been en route to the mighty bastion of Dumbarton Castle, atop its near inaccessible eminence on Dumbarton Rock, on the Clyde, when it was intercepted by a numerically inferior but tactically superior force led by her half-brother, the Earl of Moray.

Cannon fire had been exchanged between both sides before a force of Argyll's infantry tried to force a passage through to the village of Langside, but they were fired on by a disciplined body of musketeers and forced to retreat as Moray launched a cavalry charge on their confused ranks.

The battle proved disastrous for Mary and signalled the death knell of her cause, with more than 100 of her supporters killed or captured and Mary forced to flee into what she then naively thought would be the protection of England's Queen Elizabeth

– only to be executed nearly 20 years later on Elizabeth's orders.

The Baillies experienced a revival in their fortunes in the following century, when George Baillie of the branch of the Baillies of Lamington known as the Baillies of St John's Kirk, bought the lands of Jerviswood, in Lanarkshire, and later the estate of Mellerstain, in Berwickshire, but a cruel fate was in store for his son, Robert Baillie, known as Baillie of Jerviswood and honoured today as a Scottish patriot.

Born into a time of religious strife in Scotland, he became a supporter as an adult of the National Covenant – which renounced Catholic belief, pledged to uphold the Presbyterian religion and called for free parliaments and assemblies.

Described as 'the glorious marriage day of the kingdom with God', the Covenant was signed at Edinburgh's Greyfriars Kirk on February 28, 1638, four years after Baillie's birth, by Scottish nobles, barons, burgesses and ministers.

It was subscribed to the following day by hundreds of ordinary people, and copies made and dispatched around Scotland and signed by thousands more.

With persecution of Presbyterians at its height in 1676, Baillie of Jerviswood was imprisoned for four months and fined £500 after rescuing his brother-in-law, the Church of Scotland minister James Kirkton, from confinement.

Disillusioned with what many saw as the arbitrary rule of the Catholic monarch Charles II, in 1683 he became linked to the Rye House Plot – an abortive attempt to ambush and assassinate Charles and the Duke of York (the future James II) as they returned from the horse races at Newmarket to London.

The aim of the plot had been to place Charles' illegitimate son, the Duke of Monmouth, on the throne and Baillie had been approached to lend his support to an uprising on Monmouth's behalf in Scotland.

The plan had been to hide a band of conspirators on the grounds of Rye House, near Hoddesdon, Hertfordshire, then block the road and ambush and kill the royal pair.

The plan only failed because Charles and his son had set off on the road back to London earlier than had been expected.

Arrested in London shortly after the attempt came to light, Baillie was returned to Scotland, where he was heavily fined and imprisoned.

In December of 1684 he was brought up again before the High Court on a charge of treason.

Found guilty, he was hanged at the Mercat Cross in Edinburgh, while many of his family were forced to seek refuge for a time in Holland.

Another noted supporter of the principles of the National Covenant was the Church of Scotland minister and historical writer Robert Baillie.

Born in 1602 and of the Baillies of Jerviswood branch of the family, he was one of the leading members of the Glasgow Assembly of 1638 that re-established the Presbyterian faith in Scotland, and also served for a time as chaplain to the Scottish Covenanting army commanded by General David Leslie in addition to writing a number of historical works.

Appointed professor of divinity at Glasgow University in 1642, he was appointed principal a year before his death in 1662, while one of his descendants was Clementina Walkinshaw, mistress of Charles Edward Stuart.

Chapter three:

Enduring legacies

Away from religious strife, bearers of the Baillie name have brought honour to the name through rather more peaceful pursuits.

Married to George Baillie, a son of the patriot Robert Baillie of Jerviswood, Lady Grisel Baillie was the noted songwriter born in 1665 at Redbraes Castle, Berwickshire, the eldest daughter of Sir Patrick Hume of Polwarth, who later took the title Earl of Marchmont.

It was Lady Baillie and her husband who were responsible for commissioning the original building between 1725 and 1778 of what today is the magnificent Mellerstain House, the stately home north of Kelso, in the Scottish Borders.

Standing in 80 hectares of parkland, it is now the seat of the 13th Earl of Haddington and is recognised as one Scotland's historic monuments.

In addition to her highly detailed account books that provide a fascinating insight into her life and times, she also penned a number of songs that were first printed in the 1725 *Orpheus Caledonius* and include *And were'na my heart light I wad dee*.

She died in 1746 and was later immortalised in verse by her distant relative, the celebrated poet and dramatist Joanna Baillie, in her 1821 collection *Metrical Legends of Exalted Characters*.

Born in 1762 in Bothwell, Lanarkshire, her father, the Rev. James Baillie was for a time professor of divinity at Glasgow University while her mother, Dorothea, was a sister of the famous Scottish anatomists and physicians John and William Hunter.

Following the death of her father in 1778, she moved with her mother and sister to Long Calderwood, near East Kilbride, and later settled in London to keep house for her brother, the physician and pathologist Matthew Baillie.

Joanna quickly became one of the leading lights of the London literary scene, while on visits back to her native Scotland she often stayed with the great man of letters Sir Walter Scott.

Most of her poems and plays, including *Plays on the Passions*, were published in a single volume shortly before she died in 1851 in her small cottage in Hampstead, on the outskirts of London.

Her brother Matthew, born in 1761 and who

died in 1823, studied anatomy in London under his uncle, John Hunter, after being educated at both Glasgow University and Oxford University.

Elected a Fellow of the Royal College of Physicians in 1790, his book *The Morbid Anatomy of Some of the Most Important Parts of the Human Body*, is regarded as the first systematic study of pathology.

Returning to the close Baillie connection with the religious sphere, John Baillie and his younger brother Donald Macpherson Baillie were leading figures in the Church of Scotland in the early twentieth century.

Born in Gairloch, Wester Ross, the son of a Free Church of Scotland minister, he studied at Edinburgh University, where he later returned as professor of theology after teaching in both Canada and the United States.

Moderator in 1943 of the General Assembly of the Church of Scotland and the author of a number of important theological works that include *A Diary of Private Prayer*, he died in 1960.

His brother Donald, born in 1887, also studied at Edinburgh University and later became professor of divinity at St Mary's College, St Andrews University.

In common with his brother, he also wrote a number of important works, including *God was in Christ*, published seven years before his death in 1954.

From religion to finance, Colonel Augustus Baillie, born in 1861 and who died in 1939, was one of the founders of what prospers to this day as Baillie Gifford and Co., one of the world's largest investment managers.

Awarded both the DSO and the Distinguished Conduct Medal for his actions during the Second Boer War of 1899 to 1902, and later promoted to the rank of colonel, he served during the First World War as commanding officer of the 2nd Lovat Scouts.

It was before this conflict that in 1907, along with Carlyle Gifford, that he founded in Edinburgh what was then the legal firm of Baillie and Gifford.

Twenty years later, and still headquartered in Edinburgh where it remains to this day, it had changed from a legal firm to an investment business.

Baillie died in 1939, while the company he co-founded now employs about 700 people and has an estimated £66 billion of assets under management.

One of the most colourful bearers of the Baillie name was the Anglo-American heiress, landowner and socialite Olive, Lady Baillie.

Born in the United States in 1899 as Olive Cecilia Paget, she was a daughter of the Englishman Almeric Paget, later 1st Baron Queenborough and his American wife Pauline Payne Whitney, daughter and heiress of the tycoon William C. Whitney.

Both she and her younger sister inherited a considerable fortune on the death of their mother in 1916, and Olive was educated in France – where for a time she served as a nurse during the First World War.

The first of what would turn out to be her three marriages came in 1919 when she married Charles Winn, a son of the Baron St Oswald, of Nostell Priory, in Yorkshire.

The couple divorced six years later, and she re-married to Arthur Wilson Filmer, with whom she purchased what was then the rather dilapidated Leeds Castle.

The couple divorced in 1931, but Olive retained the castle, using her personal fortune to fund major renovations.

It was shortly after her divorce from her second husband that she married Sir Adrian Baillie, 6th Baronet of Polkemmet, and acquired the title of 'Lady Baillie'.

The couple divorced in 1944, ten years after

the birth of their son, Gawaine, who was aged only thirteen when he inherited the title of Baronet of Polkemmet on the death of his father.

Lady Baillie meanwhile spent massive sums of money on the renovation of Leeds Castle and its estate, employing the talents, among others, of the noted French designers Armand-Albert Rateau and Stéphane Boudin.

Renowned as a hostess, guests invited to weekend parties embraced the worlds of politics, royalty, the stage and literature.

They included such famous figures as the British politician Anthony Eden and the German ambassador to Britain Joachim von Ribbentrop, in addition to Edward, Prince of Wales, and his future wife Wallace Simpson, the 'James Bond' author Ian Fleming and the actors Charlie Chaplin, Errol Flynn, James Stewart and Robert Taylor.

The castle was used as a hospital during the Second World War, but at the end of the conflict became the venue again for weekend parties whose guests included both the Queen Mother and Queen Elizabeth.

Lady Baillie died in 1974, leaving an estate estimated at about £4m.

Arrangements were made under the terms of her will for the castle to be administered by a charitable trust and opened to the public, while her son Gawaine inherited 3,400 acres of the castle's estates.

Equally as colourful as his mother, Sir Gawaine Baillie, 7th Baronet of Polkemmet, was not only a prominent engineer and industrialist but also an amateur racing driver and noted collector of stamps from Great Britain and the British Empire.

It was following his death in 2003 that Sotheby's of London put his massive collection of more than 100,000 stamps up for auction – fetching close on £20m.

Chapter four:

On the world stage

Making her stage debut at the age of only 15, Pearl Bailey was the singer and actress born in 1918 in Southampton County, Virginia.

After appearing in vaudeville, her Broadway debut came in 1946 in *St Louis Woman*, while she won a Tony Award in 1968 for playing the title role in an all-black stage production of *Hello, Dolly!*

Host of her own American television show in the 1970s, she also starred in a number of films that include the 1947 *Variety Girl* and the 1959 *Porgy and Bess*, while top-selling albums include *Pearl Bailey Sings* and her 1971 *Pearl's Pearls*.

The veteran entertainer died in 1990, five years after being awarded the prestigious Presidential Medal of Freedom.

She was a sister of the tap dancer **Bill Bailey**, born in 1912 and who died in 1978.

Trained for a time by the tap dancer Bill "Bojangles" Robinson, he appeared in films that include the 1943 *Cabin in the Sky*, while he is also credited with having invented the dance movement he called the 'backslide' – made famous by the late Michael Jackson as the 'moonwalk'.

Born in 1931 in Aberdeen, South Dakota, **Bruce Baillie** is the American experimental filmmaker whose 1966 *Castro Street* was selected for preservation in the United States National Film Registry.

Other films include his 1964 *Mass for the Dakota Sioux* and his 1998 *The Holy Scrolls*.

Born in Bath, Somerset, in 1964, **Bill Bailey** is the multi-talented English comedian, musician and actor voted by the *Observer* newspaper in 2003 as one of the 50 funniest acts in British comedy.

Winner in 1999 of the Best Live Stand-Up Award at the British Comedy Awards, he has also appeared in British television series that include *Black Books*, and in films that include the 2007 *Run Fatboy Run* and the 2010 *Burke and Hare*.

Behind the camera lens, **David Bailey** is the internationally acclaimed British photographer who, after national service with the RAF, began his career in 1959 as a photographic assistant in a London studio.

Born in 1938 in Leytonstone, London, he is recognised as having captured some of the iconic images of 'Swinging Sixties' London, including photographs of celebrities ranging from the Beatles and Mick Jagger to fashion model Jean Shrimpton, and many others.

Awarded a CBE in 2001, his more recent work includes his 2010 collection *British Heroes in Afghanistan*.

Having performed with orchestras that include the London Symphony, BBC Symphony, National Youth Orchestra of Scotland and the English Chamber Orchestra, **Alexander Baillie** is the acclaimed English cellist who was born in 1956 in Stockport.

Taking up the instrument at the age of 12, he went on the study at the Royal College of Music, London, while posts he has held include professor of cello at the Guildhall School of Music and Drama, London.

From the Scottish Borders town of Hawick to the Hollywood Bowl, **Dame Isobel Baillie** was the soprano regarded as having been one of the greatest oratorio singers of the twentieth century.

Born in Hawick in 1895, the daughter of a baker, she moved south and worked for a time as a clerk in Manchester Town Hall, before making her singing debut in 1921 with the Halle Orchestra.

Later studying music in Milan, she was one of

the original singers of English composer Vaughan Williams' *Serenade to Music*, while in 1933 she became the first British performer to sing at the Hollywood Bowl venue.

She died in 1983, five years after being appointed a Dame Commander of the British Empire (DBE).

Born in 1967 in St Mary, Jamaica, Clifton George Bailey III is the reggae and dancehall artist better known as **Capleton**, and whose albums include his 2008 *Jah Youth Elevation*.

Also referred to as King Shango, he is a brother of the Jamaican sprint athlete **Aleen Bailey**.

Born in 1980 in St Mary and a competitor for her country, she won a gold medal as a member of the 4x100-metre relay team at the 2004 Olympics in Athens, and also a gold medal for the same event at the 2009 World Championships in Berlin.

Also on the athletic track, **Ross Baillie** was the Scottish track and field athlete, specialising in hurdling, who was born into a sporting family in 1977 in Clydebank.

His father, Hugh, represented Great Britain in the 400-metre event, while his mother, Sheila, is a former Scottish champion in 80-metre hurdles.

Winner in 1994 of the Eric Liddell Memorial Trophy while attending Clydebank High School, he became a member of a number of athletic clubs, including Sale Harriers Manchester Athletics Club.

He died, aged only 22, after suffering a serious allergic reaction to peanut oil in a sandwich.

His family, in his memory, have established the Ross Baillie Cup, awarded annually to the winner of the 60-metre hurdles at Scottish Indoor Athletics.

Perhaps rather fittingly, it was won in 2002 by Ross's younger brother, **Chris Baillie**, born in 1981, and winner of a silver medal in the 110-metre hurdles at the 2006 Commonwealth Games.

On the fields of European football, **Joe Baillie** was the Scottish defender who played for Celtic from 1946 to 1954 and other teams that include Wolverhampton Wanderers and Leicester City; born in Dumfries in 1929, he was killed in a road accident in 1966.

Also in football, **Doug Baillie**, born in 1937 in Dycross, is the former Scottish footballer and football journalist who, as a centre half, played for teams that include Airdrie, Rangers, from 1960 to 1964, and, from 1969 to 1970, Dunfermline Athletic.

In the equally competitive game of American football, **Aaron Bailey**, born in 1971 in Ann Arbor,

Michigan, is the former player in the National Football League (NHL) from 1994 to 1998 who played for teams that include the Chicago Enforcers and Green Rapids Rampage.

Made an honoured member of the Hockey Hall of Fame in 1975, Irvine Bailey, better known as **Ace Bailey**, born in 1903 in Bracebridge, Ontario, was the ice hockey player who played from 1926 to 1933 with the Toronto Maple Leafs; he died in 1992.

On the cricket pitch, **Trevor Bailey**, born in 1923 in Westcliff-on-Sea, Essex was the England Test cricketer, broadcaster and cricket writer who played 682 matches in his career.

A cricketer for Essex and, from 1949 to 1956, for England, he later became a regular on BBC's *Test Match Special*; a recipient of a CBE, he died in 2011.

In the creative world of the written word, **Allan Baillie**, born in 1943, is the Australian writer of both children and adult fiction whose books include his 1974 *Mask Maker* and the 2002 *Imp*.

Born in Scotland, he moved to Australia with his family as a child.

Author of the best-selling 2006 *The Shape I Gave You*, **Martha Bailey** is the Canadian poet and novelist born in Toronto in 1960.

In the often cut-throat world of politics, **Jackie Baillie**, born in 1964, has served in the Scottish Parliament from 1999 as the Scottish Labour Party member for Dumbarton, while in the world of finance, **Sir Frank Baillie** was a leading Canadian financier and industrialist.

Born in 1875 in Ontario, he is recognised as having established Canada's modern steel industry, and was knighted at the end of the First World War for his contribution to the war effort; he died in 1921.

Someone else who made a decidedly significant contribution to the war effort, in this case during the Second World War, was the civil engineer **Sir Donald Coleman Bailey**.

Born in 1901 in Rotherham, Yorkshire, he was the inventor of the portable, pre-fabricated, truss bridge known as the Bailey Bridge that was widely used by the Allies during the war – and is still in use to this day in civil engineering construction projects.

"Without the Bailey Bridge", Britain's Field Marshall Bernard Montgomery claimed at the end of the conflict, "We would not have won the war."

The engineer, knighted in 1946 in recognition of his bridge design, died in 1985.